Jaguars and Butterflies

Art by Ely Ely *Words by* Catherine Russler

Jaguars and Butterflies
© 2020 by Catherine Russler

Published by Bolígrafo Books
An imprint of Grafo House Publishing
Guadalajara, Jalisco, Mexico / grafohouse.com

In association with Jaquith Creative
Bothell, Washington, USA / jaquithcreative.com

Hardbound ISBN 978-1-949791-40-2
Paperback ISBN 978-1-949791-41-9
Ebook ISBN 978-1-949791-42-6
Spanish-language versions available in all formats.

Art by Ely Ely (Melissa Zúñiga). To contact her or see more of her work,
visit elyelyilustra.com, or follow her on Instagram @elyelyilustra.

Words by Catherine Russler. Contact her or learn more at
jaguarsandbutterflies.com, or follow @jaguarsandbutterflies on Instagram.

Art direction by Angela Jaquith / Instagram @angelajaquith
Title design and typography by Nacho Huizar / nachohuizar.com
Diversity and inclusion consulting by Kaila Alvarez / Instagram @kailaalvarez
Spanish-language translation by Ian Roberto Sherman Minakata
and Claudia Valeria García Escalona

Bulk discounts available for schools, public institutions, and events.
For more information, contact the publisher at info@grafohouse.com

Hardbound format printed in Puebla, Mexico by Segrak S. de R.L. MI
segrak.com / info@segrak.com

Paperback format printed in the United States of America
24 23 22 21 20   1 2 3 4 5

For every girl who
sees herself in these pages.
You are powerful.
You are beautiful.

My hair is as dark
as the rare black jaguar.
So powerful and graceful,
she dances as she walks.

My hair is brown
like cacao turned chocolate,
crafted by my ancestors
for thousands of years.

My sleek hair shimmers
like moonlight on water.

My curls are as intricate
as the Great Mayan Reef.

And my waves flow like lava
from the great Popocatépetl.

We are powerful.
We are beautiful.

My skin glows
like copper beneath our deserts,
a metal so rich in tone,
it's used to make treasures.

My skin is strong.
The sun cannot harm it.
He can only paint me
ever more beautifully bronzed.

My skin is luminous
like the moon at night,
as if she left
a piece of herself in me.

We are powerful.
We are beautiful.

My eyes are kind
and brimming with warmth,
like sweet café de olla
made by my abuelita.

Through my eyes you see my spirit.
It soars bravely and flutters freely,

like butterflies that migrate
to our sacred fir forests.

I am strong
and I am protective,
like towering trees
that shelter small creatures.

We are powerful.
We are sisters of strongest sunlight.

We are kind.
We are daughters of ancestors who nurture.

We are beautiful.

CULTURAL AND GEOGRAPHIC TERMS

Abuelita: Pronounced ah-bway-LEE-tah. *Abuelita* is the diminutive (a term of endearment) of *abuela*, which means grandmother in Spanish. In Spanish, a word becomes a diminutive when "ito" or "ita" is added to the end. The extensive use of the diminutive in Mexican Spanish is due to the influence of Náhuatl (see below).

Black Jaguar: The jaguar is the largest cat species native to the Americas. Most jaguars are yellow or light brown with dark spots, but in some jungle areas a special gene makes their fur dark all over. Jaguars are fast and powerful, and they were highly respected in the original cultures of Mexico and Central America.

Cacao: Chocolate is made from the beans of the cacao tree, whose native range spans from the Amazon Basin to southeast Mexico. People in what is now Mexico and Central America started making generally unsweetened forms of chocolate (a word that comes from the Náhuatl language) between 3,000 and 4,000 years ago. The Mayans were the great developers of chocolate knowledge. The Mayans, and later the Aztecs, used cacao beans as money, in ceremonial drinks, and in a variety of culinary preparations. When the Spanish invaded, they copied the Aztecs' ceremonial chocolate drink and added sugar. Chocolate subsequently became wildly popular in other parts of the world.

Café de Olla: A delicious coffee made in a clay pot with cinnamon, unrefined cane sugar (*piloncillo*), cloves, and sometimes orange peels or chocolate. It can be traced back to the Mexican Revolution, when it was prepared by female soldiers. Café de olla is said to have been a favorite of Mexican revolutionary leader Emiliano Zapata.

Gendered Sun and Moon: This book depicts the sun as masculine and the moon as feminine because original cultures in Mexico and Central America often thought of the sun as a male god and the moon as a female goddess. Furthermore, the Spanish language genders the sun (*el sol*) as masculine and the moon (*la luna*) as feminine.

Great Mayan Reef: The largest coral reef in the Atlantic Ocean. The Great Mayan Reef is over 1,000 kilometers long, extending from Mexico's Yucatán Peninsula to Honduras. It is also called the Mesoamerican Barrier Reef System.

Náhuatl: Pronounced NAH-wahtl. Náhuatl is the most widely spoken Indigenous language in Mexico. It was the language spoken by the Aztecs. Today there are more than 1.5 million Náhuatl speakers, mostly in central Mexico. The Mexican Government recognizes 30 different varieties of Náhuatl.

Popocatépetl: Pronounced poh-poh-kah-TEH-petal. "El Popo" is one of Mexico's most active volcanoes and is Mexico's second highest peak. Popocatépetl means "smoking mountain" in Náhuatl.

Monarch migration: Every winter, millions of monarch butterflies fly from the United States and Canada to Mexico, where they hibernate in forests of sacred fir trees (also called Oyamel trees). The trees protect the butterflies from cold rain while keeping their bodies from drying out. Clustering helps the butterflies stay warm. Tens of thousands of monarchs can cluster on a single tree.

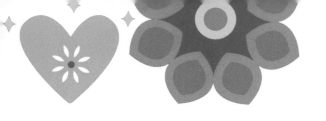

DEAR PARENTS AND EDUCATORS

We hope *Jaguars and Butterflies* brings a sense of wonder, joy, and self-empowerment to the young people in your life, and that it deepens their understanding of Mexico as a land of magnificent ethnic, cultural, and geographic diversity. For source materials and additional information, please visit us at www.jaguarsandbutterflies.com. We welcome your feedback!

For further learning and self-empowerment:

- Invite your children to point out which young people in the book they resemble. You can say: "They are beautiful, just like you. Do they seem brave? Kind? What makes you think that?" You can affirm your child with phrases like: "Wow, you two sound similar. You are both incredible."

- Help your children conduct internet searches using terms in the book that spark their curiosity. If they are not yet readers, you can help them explore images. Searching "monarch butterflies in Mexico," for example, is a fun place to start. You can explore the Glossary for more ideas.

- Use the book's text as the script for a play or spoken word performance. Encourage your children to channel the power and confidence of the young people in the book.

- Help young readers identify a culture in Mexico they'd like to learn about. There are many possibilities! Mexico is home to at least sixty-eight Indigenous groups, each with a unique ethnicity and language. Languages like Náhuatl, Maya, and Mixteco are spoken by hundreds of thousands of people and include a variety of dialects, while others are in danger of disappearing.

- Download free PDF copies of *Jaguars and Butterflies* in English and Spanish at www.jaguarsandbutterflies.com. Compare the texts to learn new words in English or Spanish. Print your favorite images and hang them as inspirational art for your children.

With love,

Ely Ely and Catherine,
Creators of *Jaguars and Butterflies*

Ely Ely, Illustrator

Melissa Zúñiga, better known as Ely Ely, is a Mexican illustrator from Aguascalientes who currently lives in Mexico City. After finishing her studies in graphic design, she worked for a few years in various marketing agencies while also doing freelance work as an illustrator and mural painter, then launched her own illustration studio in 2014. Women, Mexican graphical elements, nature, and color form the basis for her creativity and inspiration, and these things can frequently be found in her illustrations, murals, and other work. She has worked on numerous projects in Mexico and abroad, including partnerships with Disney, Google, Mary Kay, Clinique, Maybelline, Dole Sunshine, Danone, and Bonafont, among others. View more of her work at elyelyilustra.com or on Instagram, @elyelyilustra.

Catherine Russler, Author

Catherine first came to Mexico as a college exchange student. Years later, after obtaining her master's degree in international affairs with a focus on Latin American studies, she returned to Mexico as a U.S. intelligence analyst posted abroad. There, she fell in love with Francisco, to whom she is now married. They live in Guadalajara with their young daughter Olivia, ever-changing number of senior rescue dogs, and opinionated cat. They are excited to soon grow their family by adopting through Mexico's foster care system. Catherine enjoys spotting butterflies and hummingbirds with Olivia and imagining ways to help young people discover their own magic. She is passionate about social justice issues impacting youth in both of her countries. To contact the author or to learn more, visit jaguarsandbutterflies.com or follow @jaguarsandbutterflies on Instagram.

Printed in the USA
CPSIA information can be obtained
at www.ICGtesting.com
LVHW062208280923
759576LV00007B/53